# Spectrum

By Kenn Miller

Spectrum
Copyright © 2012 Kenn Miller

ISBN - 978-1-300-45008-5

Cover photo by Andrie Nel

# Spectrum

For Holland Oliver, and every other LGBT teen out there. Just be yourself, because you are loved for who you are.

Chapter 1

"I'm telling you, that sounds like the worst vacation ever." Max laughed, tossing his baseball in the air and catching it in his mitt as he walked.

"That may be," Lance replied with a chuckle. "But it's still a hell of a lot better than no vacation at all." He reached out and grabbed the baseball out of the air.

It was the last day of summer vacation, and the two of them had spent it in the park, practicing for the baseball team tryouts. Now, on their way back to Lance's house, they were discussing Lance's family's cruise of the Caribbean that they had just gotten back from.

"Hey!" Max complained, reaching for the baseball. Lance held it out of his reach, making him trip and almost stumble into the path of an oncoming car.

"Watch out!" Lance quickly grabbed Max by the back of his shirt and pulled him back from the edge of the sidewalk. Then they both watched as the car passed them and started to slow down.

"Hey, isn't that your house?" Max asked, pointing at the house whose driveway the car was turning into.

"No." Lance muttered, his attention fixed on the car. "Mine's one over this way." He halfheartedly nodded at it. The house that the car had pulled up to was vacant, or at least, it had been when Lance had left on vacation.

Now, he watched as people emerged from the car. From the driver's seat came a man who looked to be about the same age as the principal of the local high school. A woman who was probably his wife emerged from the front passenger seat. They both looked at the house in front of them with satisfaction, definitely new residents.

"Would you look at that." Lance heard Max breath. He was staring at the third figure to emerge from the car. A teenaged girl with golden blonde hair was stepping out from the back seat. She looked like she was around fifteen, a few years younger than Lance and Max.

Once the girl had both feet on the smooth surface of the driveway, she looked up. Her eyes instantly found the two boys who were watching her. A wide smile spread across her face and she waved at them.

"Wow." Max said, waving back. "She's pretty cute." He gave Lance's arm a playful punch. "And she's your new neighbour."

Lance shrugged. "Yeah, sure." In his opinion, there wasn't really anything special about the girl. Compared to Lance's girlfriend, Nicole, his new neighbour was just a child.

Lance and Max had to walk toward the new family. As they approached, the girl said something to her parents (who glanced at the two boys) and ran toward them. As she ran, her long hair spread out behind her and her skirt lifted a little.

"Hi!" She said cheerfully as she met up with the boys in front of Lance's house.

"Hi." Lance returned. Max just nodded at her.

"I'm Holly." She grinned at them again. Something about her introduction made Lance question her age. Was it possible that this girl was tall for her age and was really no older than twelve?

"Are you two in high school?" Holly asked, looking them up and down.

Max smiled at her. "Yes, we are."

"Oh, good." She breathed a heavy sigh of relief. "I was really nervous, since we're only getting here now and school starts tomorrow. I didn't know if I'd be able to find the school. But now I've met you." The grin returned to her face. "Could you give me directions to the high school?"

Lance blinked at her in surprise as Max quickly ran through the most straightforward way to get there. *The high school?* He wondered. *Why does she need to get to the high school?*

Just as Holly was thanking Max for the directions, another car drove past them and turned into the driveway of Holly's house. This car was very striking in appearance, being a bright yellow-green colour. Lance stared at it as it stopped behind the first car.

"Ah!" Holly gasped slightly. Then she started waving frantically. "Fletch!" She shouted. "Over here!"

The car door opened and the driver stepped out. Lance could see his face over the roof of the car as he turned at Holly's shouting. He shook his head slightly and walked around the front of the car.

"You don't have to shout." He told her as he walked toward them.

Lance thought there was something strange about the boy. He wore a black t-shirt and tan coloured cargo pants, which looked pretty normal, other than the fact that it was summer. It was his hair that drew Lance's attention. He guessed that the natural colour was a dark brown, but there were also patches of other colours. Streaks of a golden blond that matched Holly's hair, a green that matched his car, a blue that looked like the ocean, and even a strong fiery orange were all scattered around his head.

"This is my brother." Holly quickly introduced the boy.

"Hi." The boy said, smiling at Lance and Max. "I'm Fletcher."

"Max." Max introduced himself. Then he stuck a thumb in Lance's direction. "And this is Lance."

"Hey." Lance nodded at Fletcher.

Chapter 2

Fletcher huffed as he placed the last box of his belongings on the floor of his new room. He was finally all moved in. Now all he head to do was get his school stuff together for tomorrow. He groaned at the thought.

*Why did we have to leave it so late?* He complained silently as he sat down on the floor and opened a box. The house was move in ready two weeks ago, but for some reason his parents had decided that they were going to stay in their old house right up until the last minute.

*"There are so many memories here."* His mother had said, patting the banister of their old house fondly. *"You and your sister were both born here, and you grew up here."*

Fletcher had corrected her, pointing out that they had been born not in the house, but at the hospital nearby. As or growing up, that was why they were moving in the first place. That stupid city where they had lived before was full of people who hated Fletcher, and who had bullied him.

A shudder passed through Fletcher at the memory and he pushed it away. He was starting fresh here, and he wasn't going to let the past ruin things. With a determined expression, he started to pull his clothes out of the boxes and sort them out on the floor around him.

He was just putting the last of his clothes away in the dresser when his bedroom door swung open. Holly stood in the doorway, holding a Critter

Carrier. Fletcher instantly recognized it and hurried to take it from Holly.

"I thought he was going to stay in the living room until everything was settled." He said, peering in at the little creature curled up comfortably inside.

"He tried to bite Dad." Holly laughed, crossing the room to sit on Fletcher's bed. "Mom told me to bring him up here, since you're the only one he likes."

Fletcher couldn't keep from chuckling. "Okay." He placed the Critter Carrier on a box and carefully opened it. Inside, Bambi, Fletcher's dwarf hamster, lifted his head and sniffed the air. "Come on out." Fletcher said, reaching a hand in slightly.

Bambi sniffed his fingers slightly before jumping into Fletcher's palm and running up his arm. Fletcher laughed when little whiskers tickled his cheek.

"Here's his ball." Holly said, passing the sphere of transparent blue plastic to Fletcher. She had been rummaging through his boxes and had found all of Bambi's things.

Fletcher took the ball from her, but then returned it to the box. "He's just going to stay with me for a bit first."

Bambi was like Fletcher's best friend, other than his sister. Even though they had only come together a few months ago, they were already really close, and Fletcher had even trained Bambi to do a couple of things. Just having Bambi with him brought a smile to Fletcher's face.

7

"Just don't bring him to dinner." Holly warned, a smile coming to her face. "Mom ordered pizza. Vegetarian with extra cheese."

Fletcher smiled as Holly left the room. He already felt really comfortable in the new house. He moved some boxes out of the way while Bambi sniffed the air. It felt like anything could happen in the year to come.

As he passed the window, Fletcher looked outside. There was a window on the house directly across from his own. While he was looking, someone entered the room beyond the window. Fletcher recognized one of the boys Holly had been talking to.

The boy started to take off his shirt and Fletcher quickly ducked away from the window. As his face started to heat up, he hoped that he hadn't been seen.

# Chapter 3

"Mom!" Holly yelled from the top of the stairs. "Where's my pink flower hair thingy?"

"Did you check in your little box of hair accessories?" Her mom called back from the kitchen.

*Oh yeah.* Holly laughed slightly to herself, a little embarrassed. "Thanks!" She called as she turned back to her room. It was the first day of school, and their whole house was a little flustered. Almost everything was still in a box, but there wouldn't be time to deal with things until after everyone got home that night.

Holly hummed to herself as she fixed the large flower at the base of her high ponytail. Then she stopped suddenly, arms still raised. *Three blind mice?* She blinked at her reflection in the mirror. *Why would I hum that?*

In the mirror, Holly saw her bedroom door open. "Holly?" Fletcher said, poking his head around the door. When he saw that she was up and dressed, he stepped into the room and closed the door. "Are you ready yet?"

A smile spread across Holly's face and she spun around. "Let me see!" She said happily, looking Fletcher up and down. She loved her brother's clothes, how they had a purpose other than just covering his body, and how they reflected him so perfectly. Not for the first time in her life, Holly wished that she new herself as well as Fletcher knew himself.

Today he was dressed in simple blue jeans and a white t-shirt, both of which hung on his body well, not clinging too tightly, but he also wasn't hiding behind them. Holly grinned when she read what was printing across the front of the t-shirt. In black lettering it said 'Lets get one thing straight...' and then in a lettering that looked like it had been cut from a rainbow it said 'I'm Not!'.

"What are you staring at?" Fletcher asked, tilting his head to one side.

"Your shirt." Holly stated truthfully, grinning and giggling. "You're so confident."

Fletcher shrugged and turned away. "I just want people to know who I am." He explained. Holly could tell that he was feeling a little uncomfortable. "I'm done hiding."

The smile fell from Holly's face. "I know." She said, stepping up to her brother's side and placing a hand on his shoulder. Fletcher had felt so out of place in their home before, wanting to be confident, but always being treated like a weakling and a freak. Holly quickly pulled him into a tight hug. "Everything's going to be better now." She told him.

Fletcher sighed and hugged her back. Then he pulled back and smirked at her. "You know, you're not going to have time to eat if you don't hurry."

"Wha!" Holly cried out, looking at the clock on her dresser. Fletcher was right, they had to leave for school in just ten minutes. She ran past Fletcher and down the stairs. Luckily, breakfast was on the table, so Holly didn't have to scramble to make herself something.

"I thought things were going to be different here." Her dad scolded from his seat at the table as Holly started wolfing down her food.

"They are." She told him, taking a gulp of orange juice. She started to choke and had to pound herself on the chest. Once she had recovered, she flashed her dad a grin. "But some things have to stay the same."

His only response was to roll his eyes before returning to his coffee.

Once Holly had finished her food, she thanked her mom and ran to the front door. "Ah!" She cried out, sliding on the smooth floor in her socks as she tried to stop beside her shoes. Fletcher's were already gone, as was his backpack, which meant that he had either already left for school, or she was keeping him.

"Bye!" She shouted, grabbing her black messenger bag full of school stuff and running out the door.

To her relief, Fletcher was standing beside her car, waiting for her. He smiled and shook his head at her. "It's the first day, the one day you absolutely can't be late."

"Shut up." Holly grumbled as she opened the passenger side door and got in.

Fletcher got in too and turned the key in the ignition. Immediately, music filled the car. One of Fletcher's Devil's Halo CDs was in the player and Holly instantly started bobbing up and down to the music. Then Fletcher turned it off. "I need to focus." He said, looking out the back window as he backed out of the driveway.

Holly crossed her arms and huffed loudly. "Fine."

Chapter 4

"Hey." Lance said in greeting, giving yet another person a high five. It was just like any other day following a vacation, loud greetings in the halls, rushed catch up with friends, and tons of gossip to sift through. Really, the only way the first day of the year stood apart from the end of every other break from school was that there were new ninth graders wandering around, confused and lost.

"How was your summer?" Lance glanced to his right when Nicole fell into step beside him. As usual, her hair and makeup were perfect. She had gotten a hair cut over the break, and Lance thought he smelled a new perfume coming from her. As was expected of the returning head cheerleader.

In response to her question, Lance shrugged. "Nothing special." He said casually. He stopped in front of his assigned locker for the year. It was in a pretty remote part of the school, and he scowled when he realized how far from his classes it was.

"You can't just give me that and leave it." Nicole complained as Lance opened his locker and placed his gym bag inside. "I haven't seen you in almost a month!"

"That's still more recently than almost everyone else in this place." He mumbled, pulling a handful of notebooks from his backpack and sticking them on the top shelf of the locker.

Suddenly, Nicole's arms were around his neck and she pulled him into a kiss. It caught Lance by surprise and he pulled back quickly. Nicole pouted at him. "But I'm your girlfriend!" She continued to complain. "I shouldn't have to wait for school to start again if I want to see you."

Lance sighed. "Fine. I'm sorry I didn't make time to see you." He returned to unloading his backpack. "If you want, you can come over to my place whenever you want."

"Yay!" Nicole grabbed him again for another kiss. This time he didn't pull away. Nicole was the type of person who liked to show her feelings for someone to the world, and that meant a lot of PDA.

Nicole only let him go when someone cleared their throat loudly from behind them. Lance turned back to his backpack. "Um, you're blocking my locker." A girl said to Nicole.

The girl didn't sound very confident, and Nicole instantly turned on her. "Really?" She said in a sugary sweet voice, clapping her hands together. "That's great! Switch lockers with me." She threw an arm around the front of Lance's shoulders, hitting him in the throat. "I want the locker next to my boyfriend's."

"Um... Uh..." The girl stammered. "I'm sorry. The locker assignment sheet says that it's forbidden to trade lockers with anyone."

Lance was surprised when he thought he recognized the girl's voice. As Nicole huffed and walked away, he turned around to look at the girl.

14

He thought his jaw had hit the floor when he recognized Holly stepping up to the locker beside his.

She looked at him and must have recognized him too, because a large grin spread across her face. "Hey, neighbour!" She laughed. Then she glanced in the direction Nicole had gone. "So that was your girlfriend, huh?" Lance thought he heard disappointment in her voice.

Then she quickly turned back to him. "So, what classes do you have this semester?"

It took Lance a moment to register what she was asking. "Um…" He dug around in his pocket for his schedule. "Let's see… English, Gym, a spare, and Personal Fitness."

"In that order?" Holly asked. Lance looked up and saw her staring at him, so he nodded. "Huh." She turned her attention to pulling a stack of books from the bag slung over her shoulder. "I think Fletch's got gym that period too."

"Yeah, right after Philosophy."

Lance turned around and recognized the strange haired boy behind him as the boy Holly had introduced as her brother. "Hey." He said in greeting, nodding at the boy and giving a slight smile. Then he saw what his shirt said and the smile faltered a little.

"Did you find your locker?" Holly asked happily, closing her own and slipping a little lock onto it.

"Um, yeah." Fletcher said to her, although he was looking at Lance.

15

"Great!" Holly grabbed her brother's arm and started pulling him down the hall. "Then help me find room 127."

Lance watched them disappear into the crowd before he turned back to his locker. As he closed the door and placed his combination lock on the door, he thought about what Fletcher's shirt had said. *So... Does that mean he's gay?* He wondered.

Chapter 5

In gym class the teacher, Mr. Bevins, told everyone to change and be ready to do a thorough warm up. This surprised Fletcher. Since it was the first day, he had thought they wouldn't be changing and just take things easy today.

*Well, I guess it's a good thing I brought my gym clothes.* He smiled to himself as he entered the boys' locker room.

There were already students in the locker room. They were all talking while they changed, laughing about stuff they had done over the summer. Fletcher overheard more than a few of them bragging about having sex.

"Hey, who're you?" Someone demanded as Fletcher put his bag in an empty locker. He turned to see one of the other guys looking at him sternly.

Fletcher turned back to the locker. "Fletcher Stone." He said, pulling out his athletics clothes. "I'm new this year." He turned again to the guy who had spoken and offered a smile. "It's nice to meet you."

The guy stared at him for a long moment. Then his eyes narrowed. "Homo." He spat. Then he pointedly walked away.

Fletcher blinked in surprise. It was the first time anyone had ever said that to him. He looked down at his shirt and a smile spread across his face. *Yes.* He laughed to himself. *I am.* Then he turned away from the many evil glares he was getting and started to change.

The door opened as another student entered the locker room. "What's everyone staring at?" He asked. Fletcher didn't hear anyone answer him, but then the same voice spoke again. "Hey, Fletcher, right?"

"Huh?" Fletcher quickly pulled down his shirt and turned around. Lance was standing behind him. "Oh, hey." He crammed his clothes into the locker and shut the door.

"Hey! Church!" One of the other guys shouted. "You'd better stay away from him!"

"Yeah, he might try to turn you gay!" Someone else called.

"Huh?" Lance looked back at everyone else, then he turned to Fletcher again. "So… You are gay?" He asked.

Fletcher shrugged, trying to hide how angry the comments had made him. *Ignorant bastards.* He started to head back to the locker room door. As he passed the group of students, he looked over his shoulder at Lance. "Yeah, I am." Then he left the room.

Mr. Bevins looked up from his clipboard when Fletcher came out of the locker room. "Hey!" He shouted, waving him over while checking his watch. "That was a fast change, Mr…" He looked down at his clipboard.

"Stone." Fletcher offered.

"Ah, yes." Mr. Bevins nodded, tapping a finger on the clipboard. "Fletcher Stone." He looked up. "You're new this year?"

Fletcher nodded. "That's right."

"Well then." Mr. Bevins smiled at him. "Until the rest of the class is changed and ready to go, I guess you can just do whatever you want."

Fletcher nodded again. "If it's alright," he started, a little hesitant. "I'd like to just run. Would I be disruptive if I did laps?"

Mr. Bevins looked at him like he wasn't supposed to exist. "Oh, uh, yeah. That's fine. Go right ahead."

"Thanks." Fletcher smiled and started running. He listened as his sneakers hit the floor and echoed. Focusing on the sound, he slowly picked up speed until he was going at his fastest sustainable pace. Like this, he could probably go for nearly half an hour without stopping.

Fletcher liked running. It was a chance to clear his head. Plus, every time he passed the locker room door, he kind of hoped that someone would come out and see him go past. He wanted them to see that he was athletic, and not some weakling that they could bully.

*Bring it on!* He dared every homophobic person in the school. *Just try to mess with me.*

Chapter 6

Holly's final class of the day was Visual Arts. By the time she found her way to the classroom, she felt exhausted. It was hard enough that it was the last class of the first day filled with so much after the nothingness of the days of summer, but she had been trying not to get completely lost all day as well.

*I feel like a ninth grader all over again.* She sighed to herself, slumping into a seat at a table near the back of the classroom.

"Hey." Someone suddenly said, making Holly jump. She hadn't even realized that she wasn't the only person at the table. There was a girl sitting right across from her.

"Oh, I'm sorry!" Holly scrambled, clutching at the strap of her messenger bag as she tried to get to her feet. "I – I'll find somewhere else to sit." She could feel her cheeks growing hot from embarrassment.

"Why?" The girl asked, smiling at her. She nodded at the seat that Holly had just left. "Nobody's sitting there, and the back table is the best place in an art class." She pulled a 14X20CM sketchpad from her bag and flipped to a blank page. "What's your name?"

"Holly." Holly answered, sliding back into the seat.

She watched as the girl scrawled her name on the sketchpad sheet. She ripped it out, folded it in half, and placed it on the table in front of Holly like a place card. Then she made one for herself with another sheet. Her name was Jodi.

"What grade are you in?" Jodi asked, doodling something on her card.

"Uh, twelve." Holly replied. She picked up her card and stared at it. Jodi had used large bubble letters, the kind that could be coloured in. After glancing at what Jodi was doing, she quickly pulled out her own pencil case and started to personalize the card.

"I'm in Eleventh." Jodi told her. Holly glanced up to see her write the number in one corner of her card.

The two of them fell into a pleasant silence as they worked. Holly decided to make the card reflect exactly how she was feeling at that very moment, so she drew flowers and ribbons on it. Using a range of pinks and pastels, she added colour to the card. In the end, she decided that it looked very much like a five year old girl's bedroom design. It was perfect.

"Hey, Jodi." A group of three girls came over to the table just as Holly was zipping up her pencil case. Each of them wore a skirt and tight t-shirt, while necklaces with letters hung from their necks. They were all smiling as they sat down.

"Hi." Jodi greeted them. "Guys, this is Holly." Holly waved as Jodi motioned to her. "And Holly, this is Amelia, Bianca, and Caitlin."

"Hi." Caitlin said, flashing Holly a perfectly bleached smile.

Amelia gave Holly a curious look. "Are you new this year?" She asked after a long pause.

"Yeah." Holly said, smiling at her.

"Oh!" Bianca gasped, making everyone look at her. "Speaking of new kids; Jodi, you have to see this one guy. Apparently, he just moved here. He stands out so much, I'm sure you've already seen him."

Holly found herself leaning in a little closer. She wondered how handsome the boy in question was. Jodi's friends looked like the type to only gossip about the best of the best.

"Really?" Jodi said, packing up the mess of coloured pencils around her pencil case.

"Yeah." Bianca nodded, giggling a little. "His hair is so outrageous! I think it's, like, four or five different colours! And he's wearing a shirt that just declares to the whole world that he's a homo!"

Holly gulped when she realized that they were talking about Fletcher. They didn't think he was handsome. They thought he was a freak, a source of entertainment. She felt her throat close up a little, and her hands formed fists.

*No!* She mentally screamed at herself. *You can't do anything wild.* She made herself unclench her fists and take a deep breath.

"OhMiGod!" Caitlin gasped. She pointed at the classroom door. "It's him!"

Along with everyone else, Holly turned to look at the door. A grin spread across her face when she recognized Fletcher standing there. She had forgotten that they had this class together. This was

22

going to be a fun semester.

"Doesn't he look like a-" Amelia started.

Holly wasn't listening to her. She raised her hand and waved it around wildly. "Fletcher!" She shouted across the room. "Over here!"

Everyone was staring at her as Fletcher saw her and started toward them. "Are you nuts?" Amelia hissed. "I don't want to sit with a fag."

Holly didn't respond to her. Instead, she grinned as Fletcher stopped beside the table. "Guys, this is my twin brother, Fletcher." Now she looked at Amelia, narrowing her eyes as a look of surprise came to the other girl's face.

"I sense I'm not welcome here." Fletcher said calmly. Then he also looked at Amelia. "By the way, I don't see why you'd be sitting with a piece of kindling. Unless you were talking about me, in which case I guess it would be best to warn you that you just threatened my life. Don't use that word to refer to a person again."

Holly got to her feet during Fletcher's little lesson and then the two of them crossed the room and sat alone at another table. As the rest of the class filed in, everyone avoided their table.

Chapter 7

"Welcome home." Heather called when Lance walked into the house. Lance was supposed to call her 'mother', but he couldn't, because she wasn't. Heather was his adoptive mother. Lance had been ten when she and her husband adopted him, and he still had memories of his real mother, so he didn't want another.

Lance stepped into the kitchen and saw her rolling something out on the counter. "Do we have any ice?" He asked, walking to the freezer and opening it. The only things inside were a bag of peas and a tub of ice cream.

"Sorry, dear." Heather said, not looking up from what she was making. "Ralph used the last of it in his scotch when he got home."

*What time was that?* Lance thought, rolling his eyes as he grabbed the peas. After school he had been practicing his pitching in the park and his shoulder was sore. With the peas on his shoulder, he left the kitchen, on his way to his room.

But it wasn't going to be that easy.

"Hey!" Ralph, Heather's husband, was sitting in his chair in the living room. He had an almost empty glass in his hand. With a smirk on his face, he nodded at the bag of peas. "That your after school snack?" He asked with a laugh.

Lance gritted his teeth and shifted the bag on his shoulder. It wasn't that he didn't like Ralph, but they didn't really have anything in common. And when Ralph did things like drink in the afternoon, it made Lance question if it was even worth attempting to get along. Today, he really didn't feel like attempting it.

"What have you been doing for the past hour?" Ralph asked, using a challenging tone. "I know when school ends. Were you with that girl? What's her name again?"

"Nicole." Lance mumbled. He turned away from Ralph and started toward the stairs. "And no, I wasn't with her. I was practicing."

Ralph said something, but Lance wasn't listening. He pointedly walked away and climbed the stairs. Once he got to his room, he closed the door and tossed his backpack on the floor beside his desk. Then he shifted the peas once again and went to sit on the bed.

*Wait.* Lance changed his mind, instead going to the window. It had been an oddly hot day for September, and his room felt like a stuffy oven. He gripped the bottom of the window and, wincing from his shoulder, pulled the glass up. A slight breeze came in and the smell of the fresh air was relaxing.

Then something caught his attention and he narrowed his eyes a little, trying to confirm what he was seeing. Through the window across from his own, he could see someone moving around. At first he thought something was wrong, because whoever he was seeing was moving in an odd way. But as he watched, that person suddenly jumped toward the window and did some kind of move while in the air.

But the room was small and they crashed into the window. Lance watched, worried, as the person got up from the floor and rubbed the back of their head. Then they looked out the window and saw Lance watching.

Lance was surprised. It was Fletcher. He looked small somehow, standing there in a tank top and shorts. Lance didn't know what he had been doing, but whatever it was, Fletcher was now out of breath. His appearance caught Lance by surprise.

All of a sudden, Fletcher ran from the window. Lance stood there, still trying to figure out what he had just seen. *That guy is really strange.* He finally decided, turning away and collapsing onto his bed.

"How are you feeling?" Nicole whispered in his ear. She was standing behind him while he sat on a couch, giving him a massage.

Lance turned his head and tried to look at her. All he managed to get was a glimpse of her hand retreating. Then she was in front of him, leaning over him and pinning him to the back of the couch.

"You're so tense. You need to relax." She reached forward and picked up his hand. "Just let me take care of you."

Lance didn't know what she was talking about until she started to move his hand toward her chest. He suddenly felt his face growing hot and he closed his eyes and looked away. Even though they had been dating since the precious year, they hadn't

26

yet done anything beyond a kiss. Now that it was happening, he wasn't sure what to think.

Then his hand connected with her body. Through her shirt, he could feel her chest, but it wasn't like he had expected. It was flat. Confused, he opened his eyes and turned to look.

It wasn't Nicole in front of him. It was Fletcher, sitting there in his tank top and shorts.

Lance stared at him, not sure what was going on. Suddenly, Fletcher leaned in closer and their lips met, making Lance's heart jump. He sat there, letting Fletcher kiss him and feeling the smaller boy's heart beating in his chest.

"Wha!" Lance gasped, sitting up quickly. He had fallen asleep, still with the bag of peas at his shoulder. His dream had surprised him, and he didn't know what to think about it. He wasn't gay, so why was he dreaming about kissing another boy?

There was a knock at his door and he looked up to see Heather enter. "Hey." She said with a smile. "I'm going over to greet our new neighbours. Do you want to come? I think they've got a boy a little younger than you."

Lance shook his head. "I've already met them." He mumbled.

# Chapter 8

The cool, end of September air felt refreshing as Fletcher ran. It was an hour after the end of school, and there was nobody around as he ran on the track behind school. He was completely alone and could focus on just exercising.

For a moment he thought of Holly, wondering what she was doing. She didn't have her driver's license, so she couldn't take his car home. Even though she told him to go ahead and use the track after school, he felt a little guilty.

*Just focus.* He told himself, narrowing his eyes and watching the track ahead of him. *She'd be upset if she knew how bad I feel. She really should just-*

He was cut off mid thought by something on the track. He hadn't noticed a small rock ahead of him until he hit it with his foot. He cried out in surprise as he tripped forward. Out of instinct, he stuck his arms out in front of him, catching himself and, with the momentum, propelling himself into the air. While in the air, he flipped upright, landing perfectly on his feet.

Fletcher's heart was beating quickly from adrenaline. It was a bit of a surprise that he was unhurt, since he had never managed to complete any kind of movement in the air without hitting his head. Feeling self conscious, he quickly looked around to make sure that nobody had seen him. Nobody was around and he sighed with relief.

He decided that he should call it a day and turned back to the school. He would change out of his athletic clothes and then call Holly to find out where she was. He had to get home anyway, since there was an art project that he hadn't really thought about yet.

*How am I supposed to sculpt something personal?* He wondered as he changed into his jeans. *A part of my personality? What part should I choose?* He didn't consider himself normal, so in theory he could do anything. *Maybe a part of my past that's made me who I am?* He thought about that angle for a moment as he peeled off his shirt.

Then he turned to pick up his t-shirt and caught a glimpse of his chest. He paused for a moment. *That might make something interesting.* He thought for a second before shaking his head. There was no way he would ever share that with the students here.

All of a sudden, he heard the change room door opening. Startled, he looked over his shoulder. Lance was standing at the door, looking at him with a surprised expression. A baseball glove in his hands.

Fletcher panicked and hurried to get his shirt on. Then he shoved his athletic clothes into his bag and closed the locker he had been using. When he turned toward the door, he saw Lance opening a locker nearby while stripping off his shirt.

"Hey." Lance said before Fletcher could hurry out. "What are you still doing here?" There wasn't any malice in his voice, just curiosity.

"I was using the track." Fletcher told him. Then, taking a deep breath, added, "You?"

"Baseball practice." Lance looked over his shoulder at Fletcher. "Coach is sending me home early 'cause I strained by shoulder."

"Oh." Fletcher breathed. "Ouch."

"Yeah." Lance turned back to his locker and pulled out his clothes. "I gotta get ice on it as soon as possible."

"You want a ride?" Fletcher offered without thinking. Over the past month he had noticed that Lance took the bus or walked. He didn't have a car of his own, and the walk home would probably be painful with a strained shoulder.

Lance looked at him with a surprised expression. "Really?" He smiled. "Yeah, that would be great. Thanks."

Fletcher nodded. "I'll meet you in the parking lot then." He said before hurrying out.

When he called Holly, she said that she was already home, so it would just be Fletcher and Lance in the car. Fletcher was surprised when this thought made his heart jump. He hadn't really thought about it, but Lance was pretty good looking. He felt his face heating up at the thought of being alone with him, and what might happen.

*I'll be driving!* He mentally hit himself. That was a problem he had, an overactive imagination.

"Hey, thanks again." Lance said as they got into the car. Fletcher just nodded and started the engine.

Immediately, the CD he had in the player started. "Wha!" Fletcher scrambled to turn it off. He ended up slapping at the dash in a very uncoordinated way. Finally, the music stopped.

"What was that?" Lance asked as they pulled out of the parking lot. He was looking at the CD controls.

"Nothing." Fletcher said quickly. "Just a CD that Holly and I were listening to this morning."

"Oh." Lance nodded. He was still looking at the controls with a curious expression. "Who's the group?"

"Devil's Halo." Fletcher mumbled.

"You're kidding!" Lance started to laugh. "They're awesome."

Fletcher found himself smiling. "You think so?"

With that, the two of them were able to talk about music. It turned out that they had similar tastes, except for show tunes. Fletcher loved show tunes, but Lance made a pained face when he mentioned this fact.

Chapter 9

When Fletcher had called to ask where Holly was, she wasn't sure what to say to him exactly. She was glad that he had thought of picking her up, but at the same time she thought he expected her to need him. She was grateful that she was able to tell him that she was already home.

After ending the call with Fletcher, she plugged her cell in to charge and then collapsed onto her bed. She was exhausted, both from school and after school activities. Thinking about those activities now made a grin spread across her face. They made her feel so fulfilled.

They also reminded her that her hair was still wet. She quickly jumped up again, checking to make sure that she hadn't soaked the pillows. She hated it when she got her bed just a little damp because of her wet hair.

It was fine and she sighed with relief.

"Holly!" Her mom suddenly called, making her look toward the door. "You left your clothes in the bathroom!"

"Sorry!" Holly ran out of her room and down the hall to the bathroom. Her mom was standing in the doorway with her arms crossed. Holly smiled at her as she slipped into the room and started picking up the clothes that she had been wearing earlier in the day.

"By the way," her mom said, leaning against the doorframe. "I was unpacking the summer stuff, and I couldn't find your swim bag.

You did pack it, right?" There was an accusing tone in her voice.

Holly knew what she was thinking. "Yes, I packed it." Everyone knew that Holly had never been a huge fan of swimming. It had always been so much of a hassle for her to make sure she had a swimsuit that fit each year when she knew she would only use it five times all year at the most. It just didn't seem worth it, and with everyone reminding her to check her stuff, she had gotten mad at the activity.

But now she smiled at the thought that her attitude just might change. "I unpacked it myself this morning before I left." She explained to her mom as she left eh bathroom. She wasn't yet ready to tell her mom what she had done with the bag. *Best to give it a few more days. Make sure that I'll keep it up.*

When she had told Fletcher that it was fine if he stayed after school, she had been thinking of something else. There was a public pool a short walk from the school that stayed open all year round. Holly had decided to check it out, and it turned out to be a really great place. It hadn't been very crowded, and even though she only swam for a bit, doing laps, she was really happy now.

Back in her room, Holly dumped her clothes in the hamper, glancing momentarily at her swimsuit. She had hung it up to let it dry. Today had been the first time she used it. *But I don't think it will be the last.* She laughed to herself.

Just then she heard a car pulling up outside. Running to the window, she looked at the street bellow. For a moment she was confused. It was Fletcher's car outside, but he hadn't turned into the driveway. He wasn't even in front of their house. Instead, he had pulled to the side of the road in front of their neighbours' house.

As Holly watched, the passenger door opened. She could hardly believe her eyes when Lance stepped out. Sure, logically it made sense, they were neighbours, and so offering a ride home was nothing. It was the thought of Fletcher and Lance being alone in the car that really set Holly off.

Holly had discovered years ago that she had a distinct imagination, especially when it came to a certain genre. She loved Boys' Love novels and comics, and she read them so often that they had quickly started to cloud her vision. Now, just walking down the street, she couldn't help but pair two guys together.

And, well, Fletcher was her gay brother, so he often ended up in those pairings.

She couldn't help but grin when she saw Lance say something to Fletcher quickly before closing the car door and running into his house. She turned away from the window and ran downstairs, reaching the door just as Fletcher parked his car in the driveway. When Fletcher stepped out of the car, she was right there, staring at him.

He stared back at her for a moment, confusion on his face. Then a look of horror replaced it. "No!" He stated firmly. Holly grinned even more when a slight redness painted his face.

Chapter 10

The black seat was smooth under Lance's hand as he held himself up. He was in the back of a car, stretched out on the seat. The space felt familiar, but he couldn't quite place it. He looked around curiously.

Then he looked down and almost cried out. He wasn't alone in the car. Fletcher was there too. Lance was leaning over him, and something was definitely happening.

Fletcher wasn't wearing a shirt. Lance found himself staring at his perfectly smooth chest. Fletcher wasn't scrawny, but he also didn't' have very noticeable mussels. Lance realized that his hand was moving from the seat toward Fletcher, and that he wanted to feel the smooth skin. He quickly stiffened his arm.

Lance was at least a little relieved to find that both he and Fletcher were wearing pants. He wasn't sure why, but for a moment he wondered what Fletcher's lower half looked like. Then he shook the thought away and pushed himself up, off of Fletcher.

As he covered his face with both hands, he was aware of Fletcher sitting up beside him. He didn't want to look at him, but at the same time he did. There was so much confusion bouncing around in his brain that he didn't know what to do.

"Are you okay?" Fletcher asked and Lance felt a hand on his shoulder.

Lance jumped away from the touch, at the same time lowering his hands to look at Fletcher. "Why are you here?!" He shouted. He regretted it when a look of hurt crossed Fletcher's face. "I – I'm so-"

But before he could apologize, Fletcher had faded away and Lance was waking up in his own bed, his alarm blaring beside him.

Lance took a deep breath and shook his head as he opened his locker. He felt like he hadn't slept at all, and he was still really confused. *Why?* He asked himself. *Why would I have a dream like that? And why would it still bother me so much after waking up?* He shook his head again, trying to dislodge the memory of said dream.

"Good morning!" A smiling voice said from beside him.

Lance turned and his eyes met Nicole's. Before she could say anything else, he put an arm around her waist and pulled her close, kissing her. When he let her go, she had a huge smile across her face.

"Wow." She giggled, leaning against the locker beside his.

Lance gave her a half smile and turned back to his locker. His head more full than ever. He had kissed Nicole many times in the past, but for some reason it just didn't feel special. It wasn't that he disliked kissing her, but it also wasn't like his heart leaped when he did. Not like…

Lance quickly gave his head another shake. He had been about tot recall his first dream about Fletcher. That would have been a huge mistake.

"Hey." Someone said close-by. "You're blocking my locker again."

Lance glanced over and saw Holly staring pointedly at Nicole. *Well,* he thought, almost happily. *At least this is normal.* It seemed like Holly had to fight with Nicole every morning to get to her own locker. Lance hated to admit it, but he found it amusing.

Nicole frowned and turned to face Holly. "Well, I'm trying to have a very important conversation right now. Can't you just wait one moment?"

"Actually, no." Holly said with a bit of a laugh. Over the past month she had gotten better at dealing with Nicole. Lance had noticed the change especially on days when her messy hair was pulled up under a hat. He guessed that it had something to do with her being tired.

Nicole scowled. "What do you mean, *no*?"

As an answer to Nicole's question, the warning bell rang. Holly smirked as Nicole hurried off down the hall. Lance also panicked a little, scrambling to get his English books.

# Chapter 11

"Alright, gather around!" Mr. Bevins shouted, his voice echoing around the gym. Along with everyone else, Fletcher ran over and waited for the day's instructions. As Mr. Bevins scanned the class, he scowled. "I had wanted to start football today." He grumbled. But the weather didn't feel like cooperating.

Fletcher glanced at the door on the far side of the gym. Through the windows set into it, he could see that it had started to rain. It was raining too hard to even think about playing outside.

"So," Mr. Bevins boomed. "You'll just all have to play dodge ball!"

The class cheered, but Fletcher gulped. He didn't like playing dodge ball. It wasn't like he was bad at it or anything, he had an okay arm and he was actually really good at the dodging part. The reason he hated it was because others had always used it as an opportunity to hurt him. *How else would I become so good at dodging?*

As Mr. Bevins divided them into two teams, Fletcher scanned the faces of the other students. None of them seemed to be looking at him, and they didn't seem to have malicious expressions. It seemed like he just might get through the game without being targeted.

"Stone!" Mr. Bevins got to him and he had to turn his attention away from his peers. "Left!"

Fletcher nodded and hurried over to the left side of the gym. Once there, he looked around at his teammates. He knew that some of them were on school sports teams, so he guessed that the team was pretty good. He found himself smiling a little, actually looking forward to the game.

"What are you smiling about, fag?" One of his teammates shouted at him.

Fletcher instantly dropped the smile. "Nothing that concerns you." He replied. He was a little pissed that, no matter how many times he gave his little speech, everyone in school still used the word fag. Then he got an idea that made him want to smirk, but he kept his face emotionless.

"Hey, let's badmouth the *other* team." Someone behind Fletcher said to the other boy. Fletcher turned around and saw Lance walking toward them. Mr. Bevins must have put him on their team as well.

The boy who had called Fletcher a fag snorted. "Yeah, whatever." He turned away and glared at the team forming on the other side of the gym.

Fletcher wanted to thank Lance, but he didn't know what to say. Instead, he just watched as Lance walked over to some of his friends and started talking to them about strategy.

Then the game started.

"Ow." Fletcher winced as he placed a baggy of ice on his forehead. The spot still stung, and he was sure that a bruise was going to form.

"That looked like it hurt." Lance said, sitting down next to Fletcher on the bench. He had opted out of the round to keep an eye out, just to be sure that Fletcher didn't have a serious injury. "How do you feel?"

Fletcher shrugged. "The cold hurts more than the actual impact." He didn't look at Lance, instead focusing on his rainbow shoelaces. "I'm actually pretty used to this."

During the course of the game, a few of the kids on the opposing team had set their sights on Fletcher. It hadn't taken long for almost every ball to come his way. Fletcher had been able to dodge them all, right up until one boy had aimed for his head.

Now he could feel Lance's eyes on him. "Used to getting hit in the head?" The other boy's voice was tinged with worry.

"Um, yeah." Fletcher tried to brush it off like it was nothing. "We played dodge ball a lot at my old school." He lowered the ice from his head and held it tightly in his lap with both hands. "I was a regular target."

"Because you're gay?"

Fletcher felt his throat tighten as he remembered gym class the previous year. "No." He hadn't been out as gay back then. "Just because I was… different." He didn't want to talk about the bullying. It had been a painful time in his life, and he really just wanted to pretend that it never happened.

"Oh." Lance fell silent and the air between them grew heavy.

Fletcher listened to the squeaking of sneakers and pounding of rubber balls. His team was winning the round, but he felt bad for the other team. With the exception of the boy who had hurt him, the team was made up of some not very aggressive kids. He felt bad thinking it, but he wouldn't be surprised if he wasn't the only player to need ice by the end of the class.

"Are you going to be okay?" Lance asked quietly. "After school, I mean."

"Huh?" Fletcher glanced up at Lance. "Oh, um, yeah." He knew that Lance was referring to the drive home. He returned the baggy of ice to his head. "Like I said, it's nothing."

"Good." Lance gave Fletcher's shoulder a light punch. "And hey, you were pretty good out there."

The round ended and Lance returned to the game. Fletcher watched as the new round started. He couldn't take his eyes off of Lance, who was clearly the star of their team. A smile spread across his face as the game progressed.

Chapter 12

"What are you doing for Halloween?"

Holly looked up from her comic book when someone spoke beside her. She smiled when she saw Jodi standing beside her table. They were in the art room, waiting for class to start. It didn't look like Jodi's friends had gotten there yet, and Holly thought that might have something to do with why Jodi was talking to her.

In the past two months, Jodi and her friends had steered clear of Holly. Sometimes Holly would catch Jodi looking over at her with apologetic eyes. She was glad that Jodi still thought about her sometimes.

Like now, when she was waiting for an answer to her question. "Um, I'm not sure." Even though Halloween was just days away, Holly didn't have plans. This would be the first year that she wouldn't be trick-or-treating. Her parents had put their foot down this time.

Jodi leaned against the table. "Are you going to dress up?" She grinned, looking at Holly with wide, hopeful eyes.

Holly scoffed. "Of course!" She started to laugh. "If you don't dress up for Halloween, then you have no spirit!" She pulled a notebook from her bag and placed it on the table. "I started planning last year, on November 1st."

"Really?" Jodi slipped into the seat across from Holly and leaned forward. "May I see?"

Holly nodded and slid the notebook over. Jodi flipped through the pages, looking at the lists, descriptions, and sketches. The further into the book she went, Holly knew, the more detailed things became.

"Wow." Jodi breathed. "There's a lot of stuff in here."

"But of course." Holly had always wanted to say that. She grinned when Jodi looked up at her. "To be honest, I'm already planning for next year."

Jodi looked at her with wide eyes as she passed the book back. "So, what are you going to be this year?"

"A pop tart." Holly said, laughing at the joke. Every year she thought about it, but then realized that she wouldn't be able to move in the costume. She was really going to go as a Canadian Olympic gymnast, but she wouldn't tell anyone before the 31st.

But Jodi didn't know that. She tilted her head to the side. "Really? I didn't think you'd go for something so shallow."

"Shallow?"

Jodi nodded. "Yeah. A skimpily clad girl covered in frosting."

Holly blinked at her for a few moments before she burst out laughing. "No no no!" She had to struggle to catch her breath. "Not like that. An actual pop tart. Like, the food." She was gasping for breath.

Jodi started to laugh too. "Oh."

"And that was just a joke, anyway." Holly clutched her notebook close to her chest. "You'll have to wait for the real costume."

"Okay." At that moment Jodi's friends came into the room and she got up to meet them. Then they all sat at a different table in the back. Their laughter filled the room and Holly sighed heavily.

Holly was deep in thought as she walked down the hall to her locker. During Art class, she and Fletcher had discussed what to do for Halloween. Holly was all for dressing up and just wandering around, but Fletcher didn't want to. Holly couldn't really blame him, since she had designed his costume to not be very warm.

She only looked up when she sensed that she was getting close to her locker. When she did, she groaned. "You're blocking my-"

To her surprise, Nicole moved right away. "Happy?" She asked sarcastically.

Holly grinned. "It's a Halloween miracle!" She joked. She turned to her locker and opened it. Almost immediately, a ghost on a spring jumped out at her. She jumped and swatted at it. "Fletcher." She grumbled as Nicole and Lance started to laugh.

"That was a good one." Lance said as he closed his locker. He leaned against the metal and chuckled. "I'm glad I wasn't standing right behind you."

Nicole nodded. "Yeah. Thanks for the laugh." She and Lance started to walk away as

Holly smirked and carefully removed the ghost. She was already hatching a plan to re-use it at home. Her dad hated ghosts.

"Hey." Holly turned to see that Lance hadn't walked away yet. "Do you have plans for Halloween?"

"Not really."

"Great." Lance smiled at her. "I'm throwing a party. You and your brother should come." He waved and walked away.

Holly stared after him. *A Halloween party?* She had never been to one before.

Chapter 13

The party was well underway by the time Lance realized there might be a problem. As he mingled with the guests (making sure that they didn't brake anything), he noticed that some of them were acting odd. People were stumbling from room to room and shouting at each other.

"Hey, great party." Max said, coming up to Lance and placing a hand on his shoulder. Lance stumbled when Max put all of his weight on him. Then Max took a gulp from the plastic cup in his hand. He spilt some on the amber liquid on his Maple Leafs jersey.

Lance stared into the cup. "Is that beer?"

"Yeah." Max laughed. He took another gulp. "Pete brought it."

*Great.* Lance helped Max to sit down on the couch. Then he went looking for Pete. He had specifically locked all of Ralph's booze away where nobody would find it because he didn't want anyone drinking. Lance was against underage drinking, and he was now set on giving Pete an earful.

As Lance passed the front door, it opened a crack. He paused to look over, a little paranoid that it would be the cops. It didn't help that his own costume was that of a police officer.

A girl poked her head around the door. For a moment Lance thought she was a trick-or-treater. Then the girl looked at him and a nervous smile spread on her face. Lance chuckled and walked toward the door. It was Holly.

"Hey." He greeted her, pulling the door open. "I'm glad you could-"

Lance fell silent when he saw the person standing behind Holly. From the boy's hair, he knew that it was Fletcher, even with the thin cloth mask that ran across his eyes. Lance felt his breath catch as he took in the rest of the costume, which consisted of a pair of black shorts and a black sleeveless turtleneck. The costume was completed with a pair of large, fluffy cat ears.

"Hi." Fletcher nodded at him. He tugged at his mask a little.

Lance nodded back. "Um... come in." He stepped out of the way and let the two of them walk into the house. Then he closed the door after them.

"Lance!"

Lance jumped when a body was thrown up against his back. Then a pair of arms wrapped around his neck, a plastic cup held in each hand. He looked over his shoulder to see Nicole smiling at him with half lidded eyes. She was dressed as the same thing she had been for Halloween since the sixth grade, a playboy bunny.

"I've been looking everywhere for you." Nicole said, slurring her words a little. She slipped around to Lance's front and handed him one of the plastic cups. "Pete told me to give this to you. He said you weren't enjoying the party to it's full potential." She laughed and leaned on his shoulder. Then she looked at Holly, who was staring at her. "Hey, cool costume."

Lance glanced at Holly. He hadn't really noticed the colourful leotard she was wearing. It was covered in swirls of red maple leaves. Lance thought it looked familiar, but he couldn't place it.

"Thanks." Holly said, looking down at her costume. "I made it myself."

"Really?" Nicole left Lance's side to peer intently at the detail on Holly's costume. "It's really well done, and looks like the real thing."

"Um… Thank you." Holly looked a little uncomfortable as Nicole poked at the maple leaves on her chest. "I've worked on it since the Olympics ended."

Lance snapped his fingers. *Of course.* Now he knew where he had seen the outfit. Nicole had made him watch the gymnastics segment of the Olympics over the summer. It was the Canadian women's leotard.

"Come on." Nicole grabbed Holly's hand. "Let's get you something to drink. You have to show off that costume."

Lance watched as his girlfriend lead Holly away. It was hard to believe that Nicole did nothing but badmouth Holly when they were at school. He looked down at the cup in his hands. *Is it because she's wasted?*

"Is she okay?" Lance glanced at Fletcher, who was looking after Nicole and his sister. He looked worried. "She looks like she's drunk."

"Um…" Lance shrugged his shoulders. "I think she's had a little bit to drink, but she should be fine." He took a sip from the cup Nicole had handed him. For some reason standing there with Fletcher made him nervous. He decided that he needed a bit of 'liquid courage'.

As he and Fletcher walked through the crowd of people, he quickly drained the cup. When they came across Pete, he asked for a second one. It didn't take long for his nerves to calm and his brain to feel light and as fuzzy as Fletcher's cat ears.

Chapter 14

Fletcher stared at everyone he passed. He had never been to a high school party before. To be honest, the last party he had been to with kids his own age as his own tenth birthday party. This was completely different, and he was a little nervous.

"Hey, CatMan!" A girl Fletcher didn't know suddenly threw herself at him. She was wearing a skimpy nurses outfit and looked like she couldn't stand on her own. "I haven't seen you around before." She laughed and tried to kiss Fletcher.

Fletcher pushed the girl away, a little freaked out. He had no idea who the girl was, but when she stumbled back, a muscular boy dressed as a cave man caught her. He snarled at Fletcher before picking the girl up in his arms and carrying her away. The girl hung to his neck.

"So, what are you supposed to be, anyway?" Lance asked. He had drained another cup of whatever everyone was drinking.

Fletcher looked down at his costume. Holly had made it for him and insisted that he wear it. "A feline assassin." Holly had designed it because of Fletcher's fascination with assassins, and his love of cats. He was a little embarrassed about it, but at the same time he loved it. His only real complaint was how short the shorts Holly had made were.

"Cool." Lance said with a nod. The boy who was passing out the cups passed by, and Lance grabbed two. He offered one to Fletcher.

"Um, no thanks." Fletcher declined. He wasn't sure what was in the cup, but he suspected that it might be alcohol. Before he had moved, his neighbour had been an alcoholic. Fletcher could still remember the day he had stumbled into traffic and gotten hit by a truck.

"Okay." Lance drained one of the cups and tossed it aside. Then he took a sip from the second one. "Come on." He jerked his head toward the stairs. "I'll show you around the house."

Fletcher nodded and followed Lance through the crowd.

"Ngh." Fletcher closed his eyes tightly. He couldn't breath, and he didn't understand how this had happened.

Lance had shown him around the upstairs of the house. Each time he had opened a door, Fletcher had seen at least one couple in the room, either making out or having sex. So when Lance had come to a room at the end of the hall, Fletcher had looked away when he opened the door.

But the room had been empty.

Lance said it was his room, and had invited Fletcher inside. He had placed his empty cup on the dresser and gone to flop down on his bed. He told Fletcher to sit down, and he did, tentatively.

"You know, Nicole's the only one I've ever shown my room to." Lance said, looking at the ceiling.

"Oh." Fletcher had looked around the room and noticed all of the baseball posters on the walls.

It wasn't hard to see just how dedicated Lance was to the game.

Then Lance had suddenly rolled over, pushing Fletcher down on the bed. Fletcher had gasped, and Lance had suddenly kissed him.

It was Fletcher's first kiss.

Right away he could taste the alcohol on Lance's breath. The other boy was drunk. Fletcher tried to push him away, but Lance was too heavy. He wouldn't budge.

While he was kissing him, Lance brushed Fletcher's hair away from his face. The motion knocked Fletcher's cat ears off of his head. Then Lance started to reach up under Fletcher's shirt. His hand was cold, and Fletcher shivered. Lance's hand started to reach higher and higher on Fletcher's body.

*No!* Fletcher mentally screamed when Lance's hand reached his chest. With all of his might, he pushed Lance's hand out from under his shirt. The motion made Lance pull away and Fletcher stared into his eyes.

Lance stared back at him, but his eyes were cloudy. "I thought…" He slurred.

Fletcher knocked one of Lance's arms out from under him and the other boy fell over. Fletcher took the opportunity to run out of the room.

Chapter 15

Holly was actually enjoying herself. Nicole was being very nice, and had introduced her to a bunch of the girls from the cheerleading team. They were all talking and laughing in a corner of the living room. Sometimes a boy would come over and hit on some of the girls. Holly had almost choked on her drink when one of them spoke to her.

"You should try out for the squad." One of the girls, Melissa, told Holly.

Holly stared at her. "I thought try outs were in September." She remembered hearing all of the ninth grade girls talking about what it would be like to make the squad. It had been the same at her old school, being a cheerleader meant being popular.

"That's just a formality." Melissa waved the comment off. "We can give you a private tryout, if you'd like."

Holly felt her eyes go wide. She had never thought about being a cheerleader, but that was because she had believed the stereotype of cheerleaders were bitches. But the girls she was talking to now were really nice. She nodded. "Yeah, I'd like that."

"Great, I'll set something up for you tomorrow." Nicole told her. She threw an arm around Holly's shoulders and raised her cup. "But tonight, we party!"

The girls cheered, and Holly joined in. When one of the girls tripped and spilled her drink, Holly laughed with the rest of them. She felt great.

Suddenly there was a commotion off to one side. Everyone looked over to see someone pushing his or her way through the crowd. Holly felt her stomach clench when she recognized Fletcher. His shirt was pushed up slightly, and his ears were missing.

Holly set aside her cup and ran to him. "What happened?" She asked.

Fletcher grabbed her arms, looking for support. His eyes were wide, and Holly recognized the look. It was a look she had seen almost every day after school the year before. Fletcher was terrified of something.

"Fletcher, what happened?" Holly repeated. She was aware of the cheerleaders closing in around them, blocking Fletcher from curious eyes. She silently thanked them.

Finally, Fletcher opened his mouth to answer her. "He… He…" He was out of breath, and too scared to form sentences. Holly wrapped her arms around him and held him tightly. Almost instantly, he started to cry into her shoulder.

"Holly?" Melissa questioned.

Holly looked at her and smiled apologetically. "I'm sorry, but I have to go." She shifted Fletcher so that she could guide him through the crowd. "My brother needs me."

Melissa nodded. She turned to Nicole, silently asking a question.

Nicole returned her look and nodded. "Capsule." She told the girls.

As Holly lead Fletcher out of the house, the cheerleaders stayed around them, blocking them from any curious looks. Holly was grateful. She knew that Fletcher didn't need people seeing him like this and then whispering about him tomorrow at school.

When they reached the door, Nicole offered to give them a ride home.

"It's okay." Holly nodded over at their house. "We live next door, so we can walk." She held her arm tightly around Fletcher. "Tell Lance thanks for inviting us, and sorry we couldn't stay longer."

Nicole agreed and Holly started to lead Fletcher home. The farther they got from the party, the calmer he became. By the time they reached their door, he was walking on his own, and had managed to straighten his shirt.

"So, what happened?" Holly prompted as she led him into his room.

Fletcher just shook his head. He went straight to Bambi's cage and opened the door. Holly watched as the little dwarf hamster crawled into Fletcher's palm and Fletcher sat on the floor with him.

Holly sat on the bed. This was familiar to her. When the bullying got really bad, Fletcher had always retreated to his room, acting little. When he had gotten Bambi, the little animal had been added to the comfort scene.

Holly sighed. *I hope this doesn't become a regular occurrence again.* She didn't think Fletcher would be able to take it, and she knew she wouldn't.

Chapter 16

When Lance woke up, he thought his head was going to explode. He grit his teeth and tried to look around. He couldn't remember going to bed, but he was waking up in his own room, so that was good.

He sat up and rubbed his head. As he looked around, he saw a plastic cup sitting on his dresser. He groaned when he remembered what it had held. He had gotten drunk. Heather was going to kill him.

As he got to his feet, he noticed that he was still wearing his Halloween costume. *No surprises there.* He sighed and stumbled around the bed to find clothes for school. He wasn't going to stay home, because then everyone would know what had happened.

Lance stopped when he stepped on something. Looking down, he saw a pair of fluffy cat ears lying on the floor. He bent down and picked them up. They weren't his, but they looked familiar. He turned them over in his hands.

Then he remembered. They were Fletcher's. *Why are they here?* He wondered. Even as he thought the words, his stomach twisted. A hazy memory drifted through his head. He had thought it was just another strange dream. *Could I really have...* He brought a hand to his mouth in wonder.

"Lance!" An angry call came from downstairs. Lance cringed. He dropped the ears on his bed and went to see what the yelling was about.

He found Heather in the living room, picking up plastic cups. She looked at him and shook her head.

"This place is a mess." Ralph grumbled. He knocked a bunch of cups from his chair and flopped down.

"What was in these?" Heather demanded, holding a cup in front of Lance's face. "They smell like beer." She tossed the cup into a garbage bag and handed the bag to Lance. "Were you drinking last night?"

Lance knew he couldn't lie to her. She was married to Ralph, so she knew what a hangover looked like. She already knew that he had been drinking. Slowly, he started to pick up the plastic cups. "One of the guys brought it over." He muttered. He was ashamed that he had even had a sip.

"If anything's broken," Ralph warned him. "You're paying for it."

"Yes, sir." Lance mumbled. He wished that Ralph wouldn't speak so loudly. His head was killing him enough already.

Heather sighed audibly. "Did everyone get home safely, at least."

Lance froze. He didn't know. He thought of Fletcher. If what he had thought was a dream really did happen, then Fletcher had run out in a state of panic. His stomach dropped when he thought of Fletcher getting hit by a car.

"I… I…" His throat felt dry.

"You don't know?!" Ralph boomed, making Lance wish he were dead. "How could you be so careless?!" He got up from his chair and walked over to Lance. Even though he was a little taller, Lance shied away. "If any of those kids' parents sue us, I'm going to kill you!"

"Honey." Heather placed a hand on Ralph's arm. "Calm down."

Ralph huffed and stormed out of the room. Heather followed him, leaving Lance to clean up and feel horrible.

Luckily, nobody had been hurt after the party. Heather had forgiven him, and Ralph had just fallen silent about it, grateful that nobody had sued. At school, many people had congratulated him on throwing a great party.

But he couldn't be happy about it. Two weeks after the party, he knew beyond any doubt that Fletcher was avoiding him. When he walked to his locker, he sometimes saw Fletcher and Holly talking, but Fletcher would make a point to leave as soon as he saw Lance coming. Every time this happened, Lance felt his stomach clench.

He couldn't even talk to Holly, he felt so bad. This was hard, since it seemed Holly had become Nicole's new BFF. She had even joined the cheerleading squad.

"Tomorrow, at the game…" Nicole was saying excitedly to Holly after school on the fifteenth of November. Lance wasn't really listening, but he gathered that they were talking about some routine they were going to do at a football game.

"Oh, yeah." Holly replied as she pulled books from her locker. Lance glanced at her when he realized that she didn't sound very excited. She looked tired.

"Please tell me-" Nicole scoffed. "-that you're just saving your energy for tomorrow."

Holly smiled at her. "Of course. Go Meteors!"

"Holly!" Nicole screamed, horrified. "No!"

Lance sighed. He felt bad for Holly. She clearly was tired. Their team was the Otters, and tomorrow they were playing against the Meteors.

"Sorry." Holly muttered. She closed her locker and looked down the hall. Lance looked too and saw Fletcher standing against the wall a few meters away. Holly ran off toward him and they left together.

# Chapter 17

"Hold still." Fletcher complained when Holly yawned once again. They were in Art class, and Fletcher was trying to apply plaster to Holly's face. Today they had started making masks.

"Sorry." Holly said as Fletcher tried to get plaster around her nose without clogging her airways. He ended up shoving a glop in her mouth, which she then spat out on the table. She glared at him. "You did that on purpose!"

"No." Fletcher said, trying to hide a laugh. "You moved." He smeared plaster on her forehead, being careful not to get it in her hair, which was pulled back with an elastic headband, just like his was. "Now stay still."

Holly did what she was told and Fletcher quickly finished. Then Holly applied plaster to his face. He made sure to stay perfectly still, so she finished faster than he had. They both sat there, unable to talk, while the plaster hardened.

"This has to be the quietest you have ever been." The Art teacher, Mrs. Ayers, laughed. Fletcher carefully turned his head to watch as she made her rounds of the room. She was his favourite teacher this semester, since she had no problem with the gruesome scenes he painted, or the rainbows that made their way into most of his work.

Holly poked his arm and he looked at her. She pointed down at a piece of paper that she had written on. Fletcher read what she was trying to say. *'Going to the game?'*

Fletcher managed to keep from sighing. Today was Holly's first school game as a cheerleader. She wanted him to stick around to watch, but he didn't really want to. He knew that he owed it to her, though, so he probably would end up going. The reason he didn't want to go was because he was worried Lance would be there.

Fletcher had managed to avoid Lance since Halloween. Even though he knew that Lance had been drunk, he felt uncomfortable around him. Sure, he felt attracted to Lance, and on some level wanted what had happened to happen again, but he knew that Lance had a girlfriend.

Suddenly Holly started making odd hand gestures. She pointed at the door while waving a hand in Fletcher's face. Curious, Fletcher looked at the door to see what had her so excited.

Lance was standing in the doorway.

*Why?* Fletcher wondered. He hoped that Lance wouldn't recognize him because of the plaster. *What is he doing here?*

Mrs. Ayers hurried over to the door to see just that. Lance clearly looked bothered by the plaster-smeared faces that were looking at him. He focused on what he had to say to Mrs. Ayers.

After she was done talking to Lance, Mrs. Ayers turned to the class. She scanned over the students as if looking something. "Fletcher." She called. She beckoned him up to the front of the room.

Fletcher gulped as he got to his feet. He walked up to Mrs. Ayers, ignoring Lance's presence. He tilted his head to the side instead of asking what she needed.

"The baseball team needs your help." She told him. "They're painting a banner for the Football team. You're the best student in this class, so why don't you help out?" She handed him a cardboard box of paint bottles. "Go Otters." She laughed.

Fletcher was glad he couldn't move his face. He didn't think he would have been able to force out a laugh. Silently, he followed Lance out of the room, gripping the cardboard box tightly.

"Uh, so…" Lance muttered as they walked. "What's with the white goo on your face?"

Fletcher focused on balancing the box on the palm of one hand. He pointed at a little symbol on the box, which had originally been used to hold props for the theatre club. The symbol was of two masks.

"Oh." Lance breathed.

They walked in silence down the halls. When they turned a corner, Fletcher saw the rest of the baseball team gathered around a large piece of white paper. They were painting carefully on it, forming words.

"Hey!" Lance called out to them. "I brought paint!"

The team looked up. They jumped a little when they saw Fletcher. "What's with the goop?" One of them asked, laughing.

"Masks." Lance answered. He crouched down and took the box from Fletcher. "Fletcher came to help us."

"Great." One of the boys said, only half sarcastically.

Fletcher got to work. As the team worked on the lettering, he painted a football flying through the air, and then a goal post and one of their school's helmets. He was half aware of people staring at him as he worked.

Once, his arm brushed against Lance's and he stiffened. Lance pulled away from him, muttering that he was sorry, and went to work on the other side of the banner. Fletcher watched him for a bit, and had to force himself to look away.

Chapter 18

Holly was nervous. She was standing in the middle of the girls' locker room. The rest of the cheerleading squad was changing around her, but she couldn't bring herself to join them. She just felt too out of place.

"Come on." Nicole said to her, running over in her underwear. "You have to hurry."

Holly gulped and placed her bag down on the bench. With shaking hands, she reached for a locker that had her name on it. It turned out that anyone on a school team, including the cheer squad, got their own personal locker.

"Wow." The girl next to Holly, Natalie, breathed. Holly looked and saw that she was staring at her. "You're skin is glowing. What do you use on it?"

"Huh?" Holly touched her face. She hadn't put anything on this morning, but sure enough, the skin was smooth. She thought about it for a moment and almost laughed when she realized what it was. "It's Vaseline." She told Natalie.

The other girl made a face. "Really?"

Holly nodded. "Yeah. I put it on to keep plaster from sticking to my skin." She fiddled with the strap on her bag. "We were making masks in Art class." She explained.

"Well," Nicole said. "It did wonders for your skin." She suddenly grabbed the bottom of Holly's sweatshirt and yanked it up. "But you have to do something about these clothes. You almost look like a boy." She pointedly removed the hat that Holly had tucker her hair up inside.

"Um, okay." Holly said softly. She focused on changing into her uniform. Her hair tickled her back when she pulled off her shirt and she felt very self-conscious. Then she had to take off her baggy pants and exchange them for a skort. When she was done, all she wanted to do was hide in a shower stall.

But instead, she followed the rest of the girls out of the change room and onto the football field.


"Bah!" Holly gasped as she flopped down on her bed that night. The game seemed to drag on forever, and she was exhausted. Fletcher had come in the end, which she was grateful for, because he had given her a ride home. Now she just lay in her room, still dressed, but feeling so very comfortable.

*Fletcher's lucky.* She found herself thinking. *He doesn't have a body like mine.*

She sat up, blinking. In her exhausted state, her brain had gone to exactly what she was thinking deep down. Her thoughts confused her. Just two days ago she had practiced with the team, wearing the same uniform she wore today, and she had felt so proud and free in it. Somehow she was different today, like another person.

She flipped over and looked up at her ceiling. Her hat tipped off and fell back, but it still held her hair up so that her comforter brushed against her bare neck. She had worked so hard to grow her hair long, but sometimes she just couldn't stand it.

Suddenly Holly thought of something. She grabbed her had and jumped up from the bed. She went to her desk and dug through the stacks of random papers that sat there. Finally, she came to a flyer from the school's GSA about the gender spectrum. She returned to her bed to read it.

She spent the next three hours reading over every little bit of the flyer over and over again. By the time she fell asleep, with the flyer still clutched in her hands, she had all by memorized it.

As her mind calmed, a smile spread across her face. The words in the flyer had given her peace, and had opened things up to her.

The next day, Holly confidently put on a skirt and faux leather jacket. She carefully applied tinted lip-gloss and did her hair. Then she grabbed her purse and dashed from the room.

"Fletcher!" She called, banging on his bedroom door. When he opened it, she pushed her way inside, note caring that he was in the middle of getting dressed. She sat pointedly on his bed. "I need to go shopping." She declared.

Chapter 19

Lance was comfortably lying in bed. He was just waking up, slowly and naturally, not because of a stupid alarm clock. He felt very content, something he hadn't felt in a long time. The sheets felt loose around him, and the sun filtering in though his window illuminated the room perfectly.

He sighed and turned his head to the side, ready to doze a bit longer.

What he saw made his eyes open wide and he sat up quickly. The sheets fell away from his bare chest, but he didn't even notice that he wasn't wearing clothes. He was too busy staring at the body lying beside him in bed.

It was Fletcher, curled up with his head resting on a pillow. When Lance had sat up, he had moved the sheets and revealed Fletcher's bare shoulder. The movement had also made Fletcher stir, and he rubbed his eyes.

*Wha-What's going on?* Lance wondered. He looked around the room in a panic.

"Lance?" Fletcher said quietly. Lance looked to see him sitting up. The sheets fell away from his smooth chest, and his leg brushed against Lance's. "Are you okay?"

*No.* Was Lance's first thought. *I just woke up beside another boy, and we're not wearing clothes!*

But as Lance looked at Fletcher's sleepy face, he felt calmed. He felt a smile come to his face. "Yeah." He said. "I'm fine." He leaned in, reaching for Fletcher's cheek.

Lance's alarm blared and he sat up right away. His pajamas felt uncomfortable, and he jumped out of bed right away to get changed.

"Turn that thing off!" Ralph shouted though the house.

Lance shut off his alarm while he pulled on a pair of jeans. Then he turned to make his bed, but stopped. He just stood there, staring at the ruffled sheets. His dream filtered through his head, along with the calm, content feeling.

He turned to the mirror and stared at himself. Taking a deep breath, he admitted something to himself that he had been keeping at bay for the past few months.

*I am sexually attracted to Fletcher Stone.*

"Lance!" Nicole called out as she ran toward him. She threw her arms around him and planted a kiss on his cheek. "I missed you so much!"

Lance untangled himself from her arms. The two of them were standing in a field behind the school. The final bell had gone a while ago, and all of the students had gone home already. Lance and Nicole were completely alone, which was what Lance had wanted.

"Nicole, I need to talk to you." He told her quietly.

"What is it?" She asked, smiling. Then she got a sly look on her face. "Do you want to… you know."

Lance gulped. He knew exactly what she was referring to, and the thought made him shudder. He felt bad about it, and it made this conversation even harder. "No, Nicole, I don't."

The smile on her face fell away. "Okay." She muttered. "Then what is it?"

He kicked at a loose pebble. "I'm sorry." He whispered.

"Sorry?" She echoed. Then tears suddenly came to her eyes. "Are you breaking up with me?" She gasped and held her arms tight around herself. "You've fallen in love with someone else, haven't you?"

Lance blinked at her. For once, her obsession with cheesy romance movies was making his life easier. He nodded slowly.

"It's Holly, isn't it?" She demanded, glaring at him. "She's around you so much, it's no surprise really. I've seen how you look at her when she's chatting with her brother. It's clear! You like her so much, you're even jealous of Fletcher!"

Lance could only blink at her in surprise. He should have known this would happen. When Nicole was upset, she just wouldn't shut up. All he could do was wait for her to run out of breath.

"How could you do this to me?!" She cried. "Holly's my friend! Now you've ruined my relationship with her! I hate you!"

"Nicole!" Lance shouted, making her stop before she could turn and run away. "It's not Holly." He hadn't even really thought about Holly much lately. His mind was too busy being focused on Fletcher. "It's not Holly, and…" He took a deep breath. "…it's not any girl."

Nicole blinked at him. "What?"

Lance kicked the pebble again. "I'm not in love with a girl." He forced himself to look Nicole in the eyes. "I'm gay."

*Smack!* Nicole slapped him hard across the face, tears streaming down her face. "So you were just using me?!" She cried. "Is that why you wouldn't sleep with me? Have you been sleeping with guys this whole time?!"

"No!" Lance grabbed her wrists. "Nicole, I'm sorry. I never cheated on you, though. I really do care about you. You're like my-"

"Best friend?!" She tried to hit him again, but he held her wrist. "I don't want to be your best friend! I love you! I want to be your girlfriend!"

"I'm sorry." He said again. "But I don't want a girlfriend."

Nicole ripped her wrists free from Lance's grip. Crying, she turned and ran away across the field. Lance just stood there, watching her go and feeling his heart clench.

Chapter 20

"You're in a good mood." Fletcher commented to Holly as she pulled herself out of the pool. He handed her a towel and then sat back on the bench beside the pool.

Holly patted her hair. "I am." She said, contentedly. She stared out over the deserted pool. "I really am."

*Good.* After the football game last week, Fletcher had been worried about her. She had seemed distant, and he had seen something in her that he recognized. He had seen that she was trying to figure something out. He had wanted to help, but she hadn't come to him for it.

"Join me." Holly suddenly said, tossing the towel on the bench beside Fletcher. She stood up and dove into the water, coming up again and shaking out her hair before staring hopefully at Fletcher.

"No." He told her, quickly shaking his head. Ever since she had told him that she had been frequenting the pool, she had been trying to get him to swim with her. He always refused. He didn't want to use the change rooms at a public pool.

Holly pouted at him. "Boo!" She took a breath and ducked under the surface. Then she was off doing laps again.

"Sorry." Fletcher muttered under his breath. He sighed and rested his head back against the wall. The lights, high above his head, flickered slightly, and the smell of the pool filled his throat. It was familiar, and reminded him of better times. He and Holly used to take swimming lessons when they were really little. That was the last time Fletcher had set foot in a pool.

*At least Holly got back in.* He thought with a smile. He returned his gaze to the pool and watched as she reached the other side of the pool and turned around. *She didn't even forget anything.*

"Fag!"

Fletcher stiffened, his hand gripping his gym bag tightly. Taking a deep breath, he turned his head to look at whoever had shouted his name. A group of kids had entered the locker room, and they were all sneering at him.

"What do you want?" Fletcher asked. He was grateful that he had finished changing already. He definitely didn't want to strip with this group of morons around. He shoved his gym bag into his locker and closed the door.

"Teach wants to talk to you." One of the boys told him. When Fletcher tried to walk past him, he put out an arm to block his path. "I wonder what it could be about."

Fletcher looked at the boy with a steady gaze. "You guys are really original, you know that?" He rolled his eyes at them. *Just let me leave.*

Another boy grabbed his shoulder and pushed him into the lockers. "I'll bet he's going to tell you to stop changing in here."

"Yeah, everyone's complaining about it."

*No they aren't.* Fletcher rotated his shoulder, testing it to make sure he wasn't hurt.

"He'll probably tell you to use the girls' locker room." All of the boys started to laugh.

Fletcher froze where he was standing. *No.* He suddenly felt his body go cold. They were just joking, right? Mr. Bevins wouldn't make him use the girls' room. The school would never let him do that.

Even though Fletcher knew that the boys were just bullying him, he was afraid. He pushed past the gang and ran for the door. As he reached it, it swung open. Fletcher flinched when it almost hit him.

"Hey." It was Lance. He was looking down at Fletcher with a surprised expression. "What's going on?"

Fletcher shook his head and dashed past him. He couldn't even think about his problems with Lance right now. It wasn't as important.

He looked around the gym and spotted Mr. Bevins. He hurried over to him. "Mr. Bevins." He called out. "You wanted to talk to me?"

Mr. Bevins looked up from his clipboard and smiled when he saw Fletcher. "Yeah, have a seat." He nodded at a bench and Fletcher did what he was told. "I've been watching you run." He jerked his chin to indicate the perimeter of the gym.

Fletcher blinked at him. "Um, yeah?" *That's all? Just my running?* He wondered if there was something wrong with the way he ran. Mr. Bevins wouldn't sit him down about it unless it was going to cause an injury, but Fletcher didn't think he was that bad.

"Have you considered joining track?"

"Huh?" Fletcher blinked at him. "Track?"

"Yeah. You're pretty fast. The team could use someone like you." Mr. Bevins pulled a sheet of paper from his clipboard and handed it to Fletcher. "I'm the coach, and I know there'd be a place for you."

Fletcher looked at the piece of paper. It was an information sheet about the team. "Um, okay." He stood up, still staring at the sheet. As he walked back to the locker room to put it away, Mr. Bevins' words sunk in. *"I know there'd be a place for you."*

A place for him. Fletcher hadn't even realized that that was what he was looking for.

As he reached the door, Lance came out. He stopped, blocking Fletcher's way. "Hey." He said again. "I need to talk to you."

Fletcher was in such a daze that he nodded. "Sure."

"After school." Lance told him. "I'll come over."

Chapter 21

Holly was having another one of her sweatshirt and hat days. But this time was different. Today, when she got up, she didn't reach for a sports bra and her baggiest sweatshirt. Instead, she opened a previously unused drawer in her dresser.

After the football game, when Holly had figured things out, she had gone shopping with Fletcher. Without him knowing, she had picked up a few things for just this occasion. She pulled them out now.

First she wormed her way into an elastic chest binder that flattened her chest. This was an old article that Fletcher had given her for costume purposes. Then she grabbed one of her new shirts, a men's t-shirt. She added a pair of Fletcher's old jeans, and some plain white socks. She still wore a hat, but this time it was a black and white trucker's cap with 'We are Everywhere' written on it in rainbow letters.

"There." Holly stood proudly in front of her mirror to examine her new look. It was perfect. She felt just as comfortable as she had the day before in a skirt and blouse.

"Wow." Holly looked up as Jodi slipped into the seat across from her. "You sure look different."

Holly grinned at her. "Thanks." People had been giving her strange looks today, if they recognized her at all, but she didn't care. She was happy.

"When I first saw you, I thought you were your brother." Jodi laughed. She pushed herself up slightly to read Holly's hat. She smiled at it. "I like your hat."

"Thank you." Holly really liked it too.

Jodi poked her fingers together and looked at her hands. Holly got the feeling that she wanted to say something, so she waited patiently. Eventually Jodi glanced up at her. "Um, where did you get it?"

"Oh." *That's it?* She was nervous about asking where to get a hat? Holly almost laughed. "Just at the mall." She said. "I'll show you sometime."

Jodi waved her hands in the air. "No, that's alright."

Holly tilted her head to the side. "Okay." She pulled her pencil case out of her bag. "Hey, do you still have your sketchpad with you, the one from the first day of school?"

"Yeah." Jodi pulled the sketchpad out of her backpack. "Do you need a page?"

Holly nodded. "I wanted to make a new name card." She still had the one from the first day sitting at home on her desk, but she knew that she needed a new one. "Could I?"

Jodi nodded. "Sure." She flipped open the pad and picked up a pencil.

"Could you make it say Landon?"

Jodi looked up at her in surprise. "Landon?"

Holly nodded. She sighed slightly with relief when Jodi shrugged and drew the bubble letters on the paper. Then she folded it and handed it to Holly. Holly stared colouring it while Jodi watched her.

"Um, if you don't mind…" Jodi said after a while. "Why Landon?"

"That's my boy name." Holly told her without looking up. Like every kid, Holly had asked her parents what they would have named her if she were the opposite gender. They had proudly told her Landon, after her father's brother who had died of leukemia. She was proud that she got to use it now.

"Um, okay." Jodi still sounded confused.

"I'm a gender hybrid." Holly told her. She set down her coloured pencil and looked at Jodi. "I'm both a girl and a boy."

Jodi reared back. The surprise and confusion was clear on her face. "Both a girl… and a boy?" She repeated.

Holly nodded. She knew that she would have to explain it to everyone, so she was prepared. "You see, some days I wake up as a girl, and some days I wake up as a boy." She grinned as wide as she possible could. "Some days I'm even both at the same time."

"Oh." Jodi nodded very slowly. "I think… I understand."

"Great!" Holly spread her arms wide and stretched. "It's really kind of simple if you're open minded." She returned to colouring the name card.

A very long silence stretched between them, only broken by the scratching of Holly's pencils as she designed the card to look like what you would expect from a typical teenaged boy.

"I'm a lesbian." Jodi suddenly said.

Holly didn't even look up. "Cool."

"You're the first person I've ever told."

Holly dropped her pencil and raised her head to look at Jodi. "Really?" Jodi nodded. Holly stood up slightly and reached across the table to give her a tight hug. It was the same thing she had done when Fletcher had come out. "Congratulations!"

"Thanks." Jodi said, laughter in her voice.

"What's the hug for?" Holly looked up and saw Fletcher standing beside their table. He was looking between her and Jodi.

Jodi smiled at him. "I'm a lesbian." She said confidently.

"Awesome!" Fletcher grinned. He sat down beside Jodi. "Here." He reached into a pocket on his backpack and pulled out a little keychain. It was of a pink elephant. He handed it to Jodi.

"Um, thanks." Jodi took the keychain and examined it.

"Fletcher gives one to everyone who comes out." Holly explained to her. "See?" She held up her bag to show Jodi the little elephant Fletcher had given her that morning.

Jodi grinned and hugged Fletcher. "It's wonderful. Thank you so much!"

The three of them continued to talk. Fletcher told Jodi about a bunch of LGBT events for teens, inviting her to join him and Holly. When Jodi's friends entered the room and called her over, she waved them off and spent the class at what had been dubbed the 'Queer Table'.

Chapter 22

Lance took a deep breath, his grip tightening on the plastic bag he held in his hand. Then he reached out and rang the doorbell. He could hear the chime echoing inside the house. *Here we go.*

When the door opened, Holly blinked at him from under her hat. "Hi." She said.

"Hey." Lance waved slightly at her. "Is Fletcher here?"

"Yeah." Holly grinned. "He's in his room."

She invited him in and closed the door. Then she ran to the stairs and beckoned for him to follow her. He did and they climbed to the second floor. Then Holly led him to a door with a sign on it that said 'It's a Guy Thing'. Lance smiled slightly at it.

Holly knocked on the door. "Fletch?" She called.

"Yeah?" Fletcher's voice came from inside the room.

Holly opened the door as Lance braced himself for what he was about to do. Fletcher was sitting on the floor on the far side of the room. When Fletcher saw Lance, he looked a little surprised, but invited him in. Lance stepped into the room and Holly left.

"Hey." Lance greeted.

"Hm." Fletcher grunted. He looked away.

Lance wasn't really sure what to do, so he just stared at Fletcher. He was starting to feel uncomfortable when he noticed a furry creature emerge from the hood of Fletcher's sweatshirt. The sight made Lance jump a little and he peered at it. "What…" He breathed.

"This is Bambi." Fletcher told him. He picked the creature off of his shoulder and stood up. He walked over to Lance, holding the animal out. "He's a dwarf hamster."

Lance nodded and held out a shaking hand. Bambi sniffed his fingers curiously. *Is he going to bite me?* Lance wondered. Then Bambi set a paw on the back of Lance's hand. In the next instant, he was running up his arm.

"Wha!" Lance turned his head as Bambi took a perch on his shoulder. The little guy sniffed his nose, tickling him with his whiskers. Lance just stared at the little face.

Fletcher was laughing. "He likes you." He said. Lance watched as he crossed the room and picked something up from his dresser. Then he returned with a baby carrot. "Here." Fletcher handed the carrot to Lance.

"Um… Thanks." Lance hesitantly held the carrot up to his shoulder.

Bambi sniffed it a bit, and then suddenly ripped it from Lance's fingers, making him jump. He sat there, nibbling happily. Fletcher laughed some more, and Lance smiled.

"He's cool." Lance told Fletcher. He stroked the hamster's fur. It was soft.

"Yeah." Fletcher nodded. "He's great."

Lance watched Bambi. It was easier than looking at Fletcher. "I always thought Bambi was a girl's name."

Fletcher scoffed and Lance had to glance over at him. "Didn't you see the movie?" He demanded.

"Movie?"

"Bambi!" Fletcher cried, and the little hamster looked at him with twitching ears. "It's a Disney movie about a deer."

"Oh." Now that he mentioned it, Lance vaguely remembered something like that.

"So, what did you want?" Fletcher asked.

"Um…" Lance picked up the plastic bag he had dropped and the floor. "You left this at my house a few weeks ago." He said, handing the bag to Fletcher.

Fletcher reached inside and pulled out the pair of cat ears. "Oh, thanks." He returned them to the bag and set it carefully on his dresser. "Holly worked hard on those. She'll be happy you returned them."

*What about you?* Lance wanted to ask. There was actually a lot Lance wanted to say, but he didn't know how. He had never talked about his feelings with anyone before. When he had started dating Nicole, she had asked him out. What was he supposed to do?

While he was thinking about it, Bambi dropped the carrot and it bounced on the floor. The little guy squeaked and, before Lance could stop him, jumped.

"Whoa!" Lance reached out to catch the animal. Fletcher did the same thing.

Bambi landed clumsily in Fletcher's hands at the same time that Fletcher's hands landed in Lance's. They both sighed with relief and then looked at each other. Neither one moved.

"Um, good catch." Lance muttered.

"Thanks." Fletcher breathed. He smiled slightly. "You'd think a baseball player would have better reflexes."

"Hey!" Lance smirked. "My reflexes are just fine."

"Sure they are." Fletcher started to pull back, turning away from Lance.

Lance wasn't about to let him. He grabbed Fletcher's wrists and pulled him close. "How's that for reflexes." He whispered, his face close to Fletcher's. Then he kissed him.

Chapter 23

Fletcher didn't know what to think. He let Lance kiss him, but he didn't know why. He remembered Nicole. *But he isn't drunk this time.*

When Lance pulled back for air, they stared into each other's eyes. Bambi had climbed up Fletcher's arm and down his back to the floor, and was in the middle of eating the carrot. He didn't care what the two boys did.

Fletcher finally found his voice. "Why?" He breathed.

"I like you." Lance told him, making Fletcher's face feel warm. Then Lance pulled his head forward and Fletcher let his cheek rest against Lance's chest. He could hear Lance's heart beating. "I really like you."

Fletcher couldn't believe what he was hearing. He had never been confessed to before. Nobody had even paid him any attention, other than to bully him. The more he thought about it, the more he felt his face heat up. He looked up at Lance.

"You're face is all red." Lance chuckled, and Fletcher felt the vibrations in his chest. Lance brushed a hand against his cheek. "It makes you look cute."

His words just kept making Fletcher blush more and more. When Lance kissed him again, he was grateful. Not only because Lance couldn't see his face with his eyes closed, but because Fletcher had really wanted to kiss him again.

Fletcher wasn't sure how, but they ended up sitting on the edge of the bed. Lance let him go and they both fell back, looking up at the ceiling. They were silent, so much so that Fletcher could hear Bambi chewing on the carrot on the floor.

"I…" Fletcher started, but then his face grew really hot and he stopped. He wanted to tell Lance that he liked him too, but he was embarrassed.

Lance brushed his cheek. "It's okay." He whispered.

Fletcher closed his eyes tightly and took a deep breath. "I like you too." He managed to squeak out.

Lance laughed. "You sound like Bambi!" He commented. Then he pulled Fletcher close to him, so that Fletcher's head was once again resting on his chest. Fletcher closed his eyes, calmly this time, enjoying the firm pillow.

They lay like that for a while, for so long that Fletcher was starting to drift off into sleep. He was happy, and his heart felt light. He sighed into Lance's shirt.

"How did that happen?" Lance suddenly asked.

"Huh?" Fletcher raised his head. Lance was pointing at the ceiling. He looked and saw what he was pointing at. A portion of the ceiling was covered in rust coloured flecks. "Oh." Fletcher smiled at the memory. "It was an art project. I was working with clay, and Holly scared me."

A barking laugh came from Lance. Fletcher looked at him with a hurt expression. Lance waved an arm in the air. "Sorry, sorry." He chuckled. "That's just a funny story."

Fletcher smiled. "I know." He returned his head to Lance's chest. "Holly and I laughed about it too."

They returned to silence. Bambi had finished with the carrot, and had managed to climb up the comforter onto the bed. He sniffed at the two boys, and then climbed on top of them. He curled up on the back of Fletcher's hand where it rested on Lance's abdomen.

Fletcher smiled at Bambi. *We're like a family.* He thought for a moment. Then he thought about it and felt embarrassed for thinking such a thing.

"He's like a baby crawling into bed with his parents." Lance muttered, the vibrations making Bambi raise his head. Fletcher looked at him too. "What?" He blushed slightly. "Was that weird?"

Fletcher shook his head. "No." He grinned. "I was thinking the same thing."

Lance blinked at him for a moment. Then he exploded into laughter. The action made Bambi bounce, which made Fletcher start to laugh.

"What's so funny?" Holly asked, throwing open the door. When she saw them on the bed, she grinned. "Aw."

Fletcher jumped up, and Bambi landed on Lance's face. "Get out!" He yelled at his sister.

Holly pouted. "Fine." She started to close the door. "Mom just wanted to know if Lance was staying for dinner." She smirked. "I'll tell her yes."

"Sounds like fun." Lance told her, sitting up. Bambi clung to his chest. He put an arm around Fletcher's shoulders. "I'd love to stay."

"'Kay!" Holly chirped. She closed the door and Fletcher could hear her footsteps retreating.

# Chapter 24

"What do you think of this one?" Holly asked, holding a long red dress up against her body. It had a fluffy white trim around the high collar and the base, but didn't have any arms. Holly grinned.

"I don't know." Fletcher said, leaning against the wall beside a mirror. "There is such a thing as *too* festive."

"Oh, find some spirit!" Jodi swatted his arm. Then she smiled at Holly. "I like it. You should try it on."

"'Kay." Holly spun around and hurried toward the dressing rooms.

It was mid December, and Christmas was right around the corner. Holly, Fletcher, and Jodi were all at the mall for last minute shopping, which didn't just have to be gifts. Holly was determined to find the perfect Christmas dress. It was her first Christmas in this town, and she planned to spread her spirit.

When she got the dress on, Holly looked in the mirror. She frowned at her reflection. *Maybe not.* It did look a little tacky. She decided to get more opinions on it and stepped out of the stall.

"It fits you well." Jodi said, giving her a thumbs up.

Fletcher frowned and shook his head. "I don't like it."

"I know." Holly turned around slowly, looking over her shoulder at the back of the dress. "It looks like a sandwich, right?"

Fletcher nodded. Then he stepped up to her and crouched and her feet. He started to examine the fluff at the bottom of the dress. Holly saw a mischievous smile touch his face. "You know, this is only attached by a thin threat about ever five centimeters." He looked up at her. "You could cut it off."

Holly frowned. That wouldn't really do much for the dress. Then she brightened when she realized what Fletcher was thinking. "And turn it into a belt!"

"Exactly."

Holly jumped up and down. "Okay!" She dashed back into the dressing room to take the dress off. From inside, she could hear Fletcher and Jodi talking.

"Do you two always shop like this?" Jodi asked Fletcher.

"Yeah." Fletcher said, and Holly could see him shrugging his shoulders. "If you can't find *exactly* what your looking for, there's no rule that says you can't buy something an alter it."

"Is that why Holly has such strange clothes?"

"I heard that!" Holly shouted. She laughed. "And yes, it is."

She left the dressing room and the three of them headed to the cash. While Holly paid for the dress, Fletcher and Jodi examined the little trinkets on display in the front counter. They were all Christmas themed jewelry.

"Do you think Mac would like those?" Jodi asked. Holly looked to see that she was pointing at pair of little reindeer earrings. The sign said that they lit up.

Fletcher started to laugh. "I don't see why she wouldn't."

Holly smiled and stepped aside to let Jodi buy the earrings.

When she and Fletcher had taken Jodi to her first LGBT event at the end of November, Jodi had met a girl there named Madeline Connors. They had instantly hit it off, and Jodi said they talked online every single day. Mac was a first year in University, so she was two years older than Jodi, but they had so much in common that Holly didn't find it hard at all to see them as a couple.

They left the store and continued walking though the mall. Fletcher kept stopping every time they passed a sports store. Eventually, Holly stopped him.

"Just get him a new baseball!" She cried. The only gift Fletcher had yet to buy was Lance's, and it was driving Holly crazy.

Like every time Holly made a suggestion about the gift, Fletcher shook his head. "It's not personal enough."

Holly huffed in frustration.

"Why don't you get him a rainbow baseball?" Jodi offered. "You're at that stage where you give a joke gift."

Fletcher started to shake his head, but then paused. "Where would I get one?" He asked.

Holly perked up. "I know! I know!" She grabbed Fletcher's hand and started pulling him through the mall. Jodi ran after them. Holly was grinning from ear to ear as she turned a corner and pulled her brother into her favourite store. It was where she had gotten her collection of awesome trucker caps.

"Can I help you?" The boy behind the counter asked. Holly looked at him and saw that he was a little scared. Then he recognized her and laughed. "Holly. It's good to see you."

"Hi Zeke!" She walked up to the counter and leaned against it. "Actually, we do need help." She pointed at Fletcher. "My brother just got his first boyfriend, and he's looking for the right gift. Do you have a rainbow baseball?"

Zeke looked over Holly's shoulder at Fletcher and laughed. "Of course we do." He ducked into the back of the room and returned almost instantly with a small box. "Here." He placed it on the counter.

Then he leaned closer to whisper in her ear. "And I wanted to thank you for that print out. It made talking with my parents really easy."

Holly grinned. "No prob."

Zeke was a gender hybrid like her. They had actually met just after Holly had reached the truth about herself. Zeke had helped her, so when he admitted that his parents didn't know what he was, Holly had given him advice.

"Hey," Zeke winked at her. "Will I see you at the Christmas party."

"Yup." Holly held up her most recent purchase. "And I just got an amazing dress."

"I hope I get to see it." Zeke laughed.

Chapter 25

Christmas Eve. Lance inhaled deeply, breathing in the incense that Heather always burned this time of year. It made the whole house smell like a log cabin. Usually he didn't like it, because it felt stuffy, but this year it made him smile.

The doorbell rang and Lance jumped up from the couch. Heather and Ralph were off at some Christmas party with their friends, so he had the house to himself. That was good, because he hadn't yet told them that he was gay.

"Hey." Lance grinned when he opened the door and saw Fletcher standing there.

"Hi." Fletcher smiled back. He looked kind of like Bambi, wearing a fuzzy hat and mitts. He held out a small present to Lance. "Here."

Lance took Fletcher's wrist and pulled him inside and into a kiss. He closed the door and pulled the hat from Fletcher's head. "You didn't have to get me anything." He whispered.

Fletcher blushed. "I wanted to."

Lance helped Fletcher to take off his coat and boots. Then he led him into the living room. They sat down together on the couch and Lance picked up a gift bag. "Well, I got you something too." He said, passing it to Fletcher.

Fletcher held the bag in his hands and stared at it. Then he looked up at Lance. "Really?"

"It's not an illusion." Lance laughed. "Open it."

Lance nervously watched as Fletcher reached inside the bag. He had thought long and hard about what to get for him. When he and Nicole had shared a Christmas, all she had wanted was jewelry. Lance knew that he had to get something more personal for Fletcher.

As Fletcher pulled out the tissue paper wrapped object, Lance grinned. He watched as Fletcher tore away the paper and held up the book.

"Socrates?" Fletcher looked up at him. He was smiling and Lance breathed a sigh a relief.

"Yeah." Lance scratched the back of his neck. "I remembered that you said you were taking Philosophy, so I thought you might like it."

"Thank you." Fletcher leaned forward and kissed Lance. "Now open yours."

Lance nodded and tore the bright paper off of the cube in his hands. He laughed out loud when he saw the box. "Really?" He opened it and picked up the bright baseball. "It's so cool." He started tossing it in the air. "I can't believe they even make these."

Fletcher grinned at him. "You just need to know where to look."

Lance wrapped his arms around Fletcher and kissed him deeply. The stupid Christmas specials were right; it was a very romantic time of year. He just couldn't help himself; he leaned in, pushing Fletcher onto his back.

"Lance?" Fletcher gasped.

"I love you." Lance whispered in his ear. He kissed him again. He could feel Fletcher fumbling with the buttons on his shirt, so he reached for Fletcher's shirt. For a moment his dreams floated through his head, and he remembered how he had stared at Fletcher's perfect chest. He got excited thinking about seeing the real thing.

"Wait!" Fletcher suddenly gasped, just as Lance was about to pull his shirt off. He sat up and backed away from Lance. He was holding his arms across his chest, holding his shirt down.

"What is it?"

Fletcher wouldn't look at him. "I… I don't want you to see." He whispered. He sounded embarrassed. "You… you won't…"

Lance reached out a hand and brushed Fletcher's cheek. "I won't what?" He asked softly. He didn't know what Fletcher was embarrassed about, but he was sure, whatever it was, he would love Fletcher more for it.

Fletcher shook his head. "You don't want to see!" He said firmly.

Lance kissed him softly. "Let me see." He whispered.

Fletcher hesitated, but then he nodded. Lance watched as he slowly pulled up his shirt. He pulled it over his head and then held it tightly in his lap. He wouldn't look at Lance again.

Lance blinked in surprise. Fletcher's chest wasn't smooth like he ad expected. He had two long scars that ran from the center of his chest to under his arms. They looked kind of new, like they were less than a year old. Lance didn't know what they could be from, but he guessed that they had hurt.

He reached out a shaking hand. "May I?" He asked.

Fletcher nodded and Lace laid a hand on one of the scars. It was smooth, well healed. Lance smiled slightly. He thought it was cute that Fletcher was embarrassed about a couple of scars.

# Chapter 26

Fletcher shuddered. Lance's hand felt cold against his skin. The only person who had ever touched those scars before was the doctor Fletcher had seen before he moved. He had done whatever he could to hide them from people.

"What are they from?" Lance asked.

Fletcher stiffened. *Why did he have to ask?* He knew that it was a natural question, but Fletcher dreaded having to answer. He felt tears come to his eyes. He was scared of how Lance would react.

"Fletcher?" Lance pulled him close and turned his head to look at him. "You're crying."

He pulled away and whipped his eyes. "Um, yeah. Sorry." He took a deep breath to calm himself. "I just... um... I'm scared." He whispered.

"Scared of what?"

Fletcher gulped. "Scared you'll hate me if I tell you." He griped his shirt tightly, his stomach clenching even tighter.

"I could never hate you." Lance said. Then he kissed him again. "Don't ever think that."

Fletcher let go of his shirt and grabbed Lance's wrists. He pushed him back to arms length before letting go. He looked down at his lap. "You can't promise that." He took another deep breath and forced himself to look Lance in the eye. "I'm transgender."

Silence followed. They just stared at each other. With each passing moment, Fletcher's heart tightened. He could see the surprise in Lance's eyes, and could only imagine the thoughts that were running through his head.

They would be the same thoughts that were shouted at Fletcher last year after he came out. He could still hear them when he closed his eyes at night. They haunted him, and he was terrified now that he would hear the same things from Lance.

Finally, Lance spoke. "Transgender?" He breathed. "I don't understand."

Fletcher started to shake. He knew that he was about to start crying, for real this time. "I – I'm a boy!" He cried. "But… I was born in a female body."

The truth was, he and Holly were identical twins. They had grown up looking like carbon copies of each other. But it had been perfectly clear to Fletcher that something was wrong. He wasn't right. He wasn't a girl!

Fletcher covered his eyes and cried. He felt pathetic. Here he was, in someone else's house, sharing his deepest secret, and bawling. But he just couldn't stop.

"Hey, hey, hey." Lance said softly, and Fletcher was pulled toward him. He felt a hand on his head. "Don't cry like that. Shh. I understand. It's alright."

Lance's soft voice was calming. Fletcher felt his tears slow, and he stared gasping slightly, trying to stop them completely. He buried his face in Lance's chest, grateful.

"You don't have to explain anything to me." Lance whispered in his ear. "I understand, and

I'm honored that you told me." Fletcher felt him press his lips to the top of his head. "Thank you." He murmured.

Fletcher wrapped his arms around Lance and gripped the back of his shirt tightly. He was so happy that Lance hadn't pushed him away when he had found out. Relief flooded over him, and he suddenly felt very tiered.

"Come on." Lance said. He got up from the couch and pulled Fletcher up beside him. "You can spend the night." He smiled, and Fletcher smiled back.

He followed Lance up the stairs and into the same room he had been in on Halloween. Lance walked over to the dresser and opened one of the drawers. He pulled out a pair of pajamas.

"Here." He handed the pajamas to Fletcher. "You can borrow these."

Fletcher nodded and Lance ducked into the hall with another pair. As fast as he could, Fletcher changed into the pajamas. They were a bit big on him, and the sleeves slid past his hands. He smiled though, and hugged himself tightly.

When Lance came back, he smiled at Fletcher. "They look good on you." He said with a laugh.

Fletcher laughed too. Then they got into the bed together. Under the sheets, Fletcher crawled close to Lance. When Lance put an arm around him, he placed his head on his chest. He was very comfortable, and quickly fell asleep.

www.ingramcontent.com/pod-product-compliance
Lightning Source LLC
Chambersburg PA
CBHW070834310526
45788CB00017B/988